WHOLENESS IN GOD

WOMEN'S GROUP BIBLE STUDY

WRITTEN BY Sharon Bernhardt

RELEVANCE SERIES

Wholeness in God: Women's Group Bible Study

Written by Sharon Bernhardt

Requests for information should be sent to:

Warner Press Inc.

P.O. Box 2499

Anderson, IN 46018

www.warnerpress.org

Kevin Stiffler • Editor

S. Katie Miller • Layout & Design

CONTENTS

The Warner Press *Relevance* Group Bible Studies provide intriguing examinations of topics using the whole of the Scriptures. The guides incorporate various stories and activities to introduce and apply the subject matter, with a Bible study component at the heart of each session. Our goal is to show life-long believers and those new to the faith how to know the Lord intimately while encouraging them to step out and join him in his work with miraculous results.

These flexible studies are ideal for any setting. We know that time is a valuable commodity in today's society, and that's why each book consists of five or six short lessons intended to meet the group's scheduling needs.

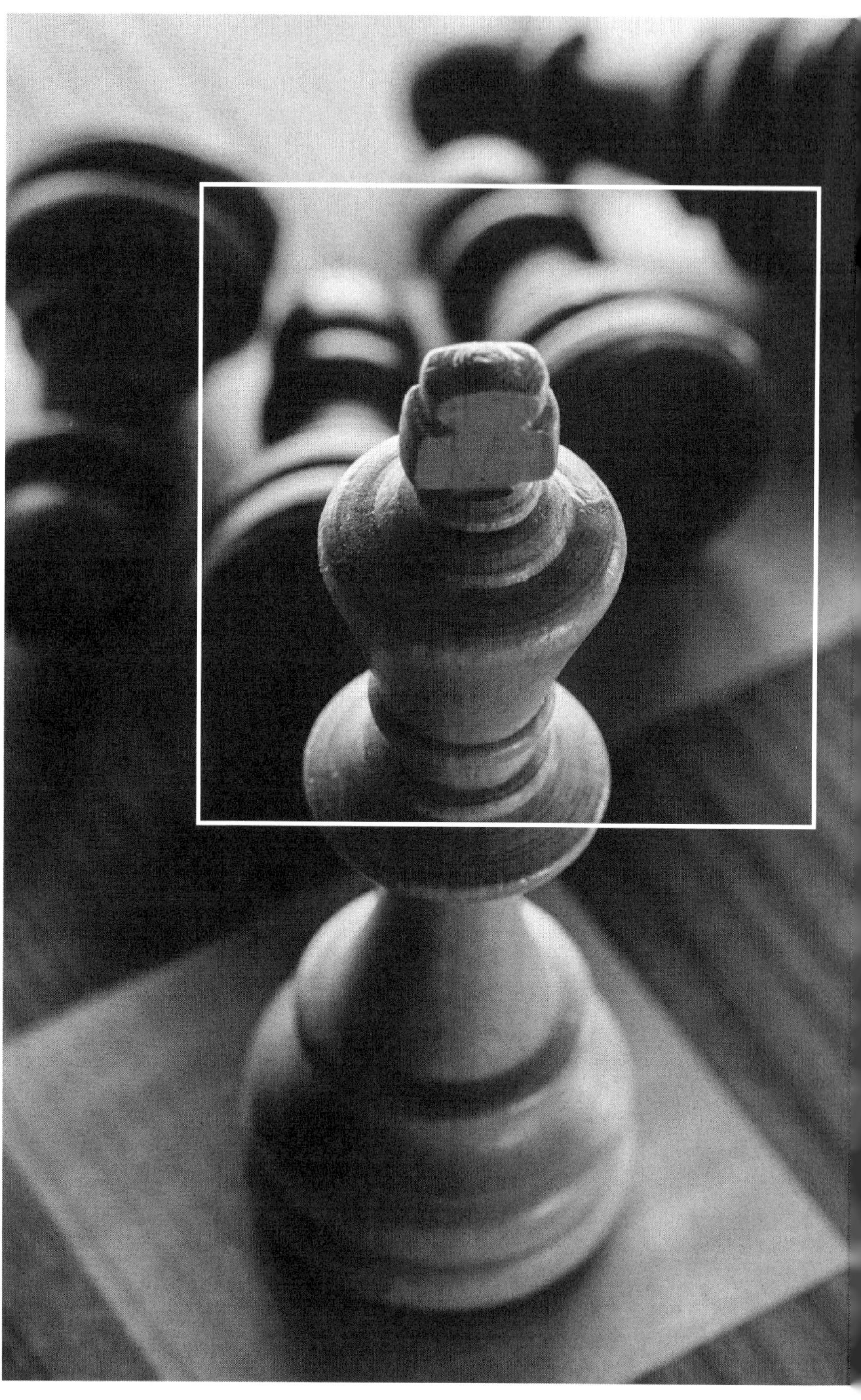

L1

No Excuses

1 Samuel 15

Main Point

King Saul discovered the necessity of following God's commands.

Background

When the Israelites left Egypt, they embarked on a perilous journey. Running from their enemies into the inhospitable and treacherous desert, their prospects looked grim. God had delivered them from Pharaoh's clutches and would continue to provide for them, but the trek seemed all too daunting. In the midst of this challenging journey, the Amalekites confronted the Lord's people. They attacked the exhausted Israelites and struck down those who were defenseless (Deut 25:17–19). God promised vengeance and gave King Saul the job to mete out the consequences. Saul's instructions were to completely annihilate those who had attacked God's chosen people in their time of weakness

Traffic and Consequences

Westerners who travel to countries in Asia and Africa sometimes feel a sense of surprise and frustration when they get behind the wheel. Drivers there rarely follow the rules of the road; they just seem to go where they want to, when they want to. Westerners who attempt to drive in the way they were taught or try to drive by the posted instructions can be at a greater risk for accident, for they are not "flowing" with the other vehicles. Those who don't take the opportunity to forge into traffic and cut other drivers off can get stuck for a long time, waiting to politely merge. Drivers have to be extra diligent and aware so that they don't have an accident because everyone is driving as they believe to be best, without regard for the rules.

What situations have you encountered where inconsiderate people caused problems for others by their choices?

What are the benefits of having rules or instructions in society?

Are you a person who religiously follows the rules or do you struggle to do so if you think another way is better? Why?

I. Read 1 Samuel 15:1–9.

Samuel brought a message to Saul, giving him instructions from the Lord. He also reminded Saul about who Saul was and what role God had given him. Why do you think this was necessary?

What task did God charge Saul with? Why did the Lord want to take these steps? Why do you think God told Saul to take such drastic action?

The Lord's retribution on the Amalekites took over four hundred years to occur. No one who had experienced the attack by the Amalekites was even alive. Sometimes God's response is not in our timing, but the Lord is faithful. Describe an experience when you waited a long time for God's response to a problem or God's help in a situation. What enabled you to persevere as you waited?

What did King Saul and his men do? Why do you think they did this? How was this in conflict with the instructions God gave?

II. Read 1 Samuel 15:10–23.

What was Samuel's reaction when he heard that God was disappointed in Saul? Why do you think he felt this way? Describe a time when you felt sad for someone who had sinned.

When Samuel went to find Saul, what was Saul doing? In what manner did Saul greet Samuel? What does this tell us about Saul's frame of mind after the battle?

What was Saul's report to Samuel? When Samuel confronted him, what was Saul's response? Saul believed he had good reasons for the decisions he made, even though they were against God's instructions. Describe a time you chose to do something your way, even though God told you to do something differently. What was the result?

What did Samuel explain to Saul about God's desires for God's people? What does this say to us about what God expects of us today?

III. Read 1 Samuel 15:24–31.

How did Saul react when he finally understood what Samuel was saying? In his statements of contrition, who did he seem to be most concerned about? What was Samuel's response to Saul? Why do you think he responded in this way?

IV. Read 1 Samuel 15:32–35.

What was King Agag's demeanor when he was brought before Samuel? Why do you think he had that response? Who executed King Agag? What does this suggest?

What happened to the relationship between Saul and Samuel? Why do you think this occurred? Describe a time you had a similar experience with someone.

What can we learn from Saul's experience?

What God Sees

Saul was an imposing person who looked like a king. When the people spoke up and told Samuel that they were dissatisfied and wanted a king, they were impressed with God's choice. Saul's physical appearance was kingly, but his heart and character were a disappointment. He did not follow God's instructions and he sought to glorify himself. Saul's choices angered the Lord and grieved Samuel. God led Samuel to Jesse's home and showed him that a young shepherd boy was God's choice. When the young David was anointed to take over from Saul, Samuel felt uncertain about God's decision. But the Lord reminded Samuel that God sees within the heart. God is the one who knows our hearts and our motivations. God knows when we are seeking to glorify ourselves, and God knows when our confession and our contrition are genuine rather than self-serving. God is the judge who knows our hearts.

Have you ever misjudged someone? How did you find out the truth about this person's character? What caused you to "miss the mark" in your estimation?

Pressure and Influence

When Saul finally admitted that he had done something wrong, he stated that he had made that choice because he had been afraid of the people. He had let the influence of others keep him from obeying God. Although Saul was king, he bent to the will of the people instead of standing firmly with the Lord.

External peer pressure can be a strong force. When others share good ideas, it can be hard to stand against them. The people wanted to keep the best of the sheep, goats, cattle, and plunder to sacrifice to the Lord. This seemed like a proper and fitting thing to do, so Saul bent to their will even though his instructions from the Lord had been different. In today's culture it is easy to be influenced by the latest interpretations of the Scriptures and the latest trends—even in the church. It can be uncomfortable to stand against the crowd and do what God has commanded.

What influences have you experienced from outside or even within the church? How have you been successful or unsuccessful in standing firm in the Lord? What has been the greatest challenge you have faced in this area?

Reflection and Repentance

Sometimes we call out for an answer to prayer or for guidance and direction, but the Lord is silent. This can leave us frustrated and confused, and it may cause us even to doubt God's existence. When we are in such situations, we need to carefully examine our hearts and bring ourselves to God in reflection and repentance. In Psalm 26:2, David prayed, "Test me, LORD, and try me, examine my heart and my mind," and in Psalm 51:10, "Create in me a pure heart, O God, and renew a steadfast spirit within me."

It seems that Saul never completely repented in his heart; he only said sorry when Samuel cornered him. Saul never regained a close and intimate relationship with God where God directed his paths and walked with him. David, on the other hand, continually asked God to examine him and renew his heart and mind. When he sinned, he sought to restore his relationship with the Lord.

When we ask God to examine our hearts, what do we need to be prepared to do in response?

What does it mean to have a "pure heart" and a "steadfast spirit"? Describe the lifestyle and behavior of such people.

Closing Prayer

Dear Lord, your Word promises that you will forgive our sins and cleanse us from unrighteousness when we confess our sins to you. Forgive us for times when we have chosen to go our own way. Forgive us for times when we heard your voice but thought we knew better. Help us remember that you know what is best for us and that we should follow you always. Restore us to right relationship with you, we pray. Amen. ■

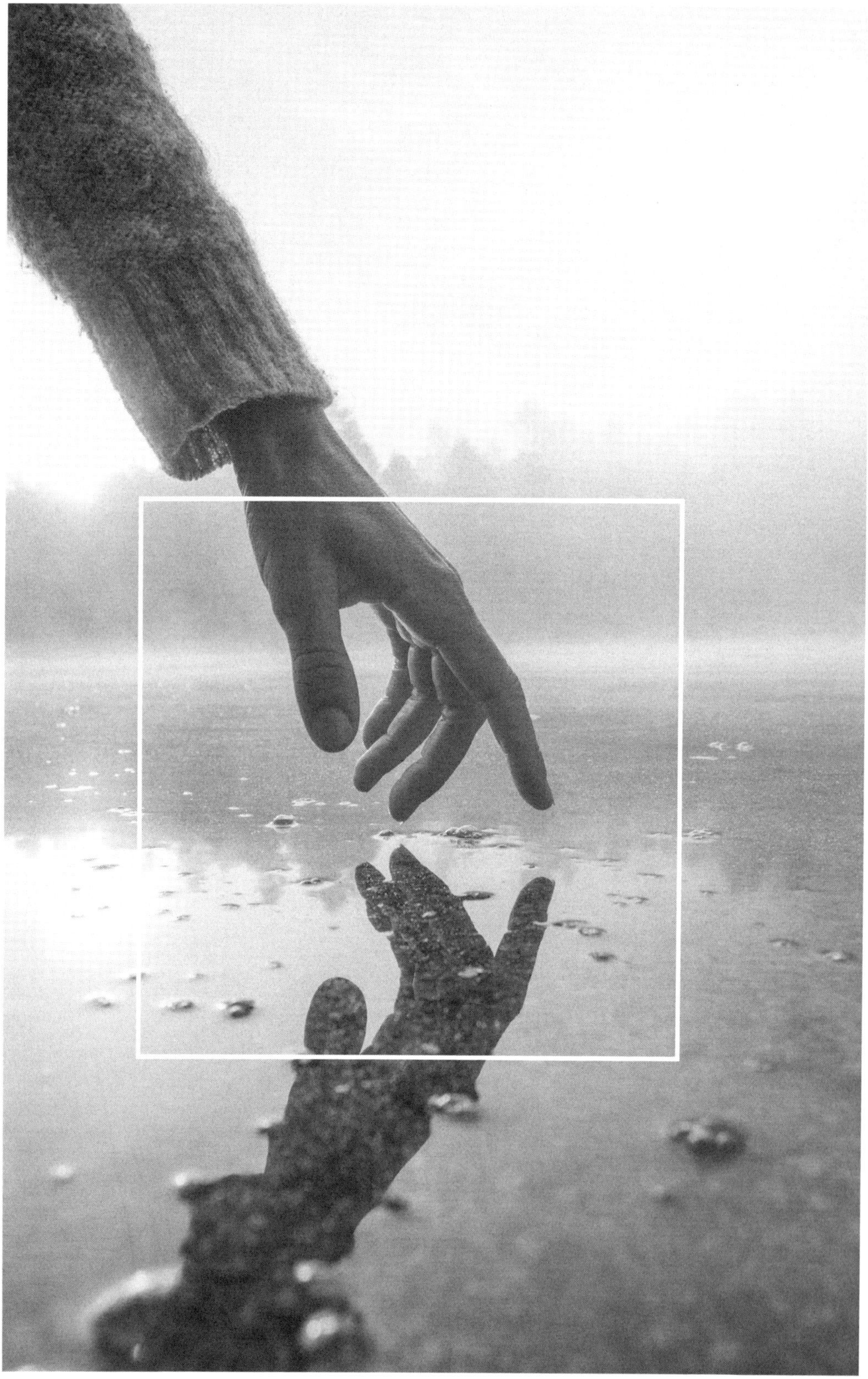

L2

Do You Want to Be Healed?

John 5:1–15

Main Point

Jesus offers healing and a path out of victimization.

Background

The pool of Bethesda was located near the Sheep Gate in Jerusalem. The word *Bethesda* means "House of Mercy" or "House of Grace." This pool had a unique function; it was a place where the injured, diseased, or infirm could come to receive healing. Five porticos surrounded the pool and the sick would rest there, waiting for the water to stir. Whenever the water in the pool was occasionally stirred (presumably by an angel), the first person who managed to get into the water at that time would be healed of whatever condition he or she had. One man missed getting into the pool first but was healed by Jesus instead.

Wants and Needs

Since the fall of Adam and Eve, humans have been disconnected from God. This brokenness has produced a longing for fulfillment that is not fully quenchable. The separation will continue until we are in God's presence once more. In the meantime, humans seek to fill their hearts with insufficient things: food, sex, relationships, alcohol, drugs, and other crutches. Sadly, people don't even recognize what it is that they really need. But God sees the heart. God knows each person's inmost being—exactly what we are missing and how it is God that we need most of all. God knows that we try to fill up our hearts and minds with other things, many of which are not good for us. God wants us to recognize that our true need is for God, to long for and desire relationship and intimacy with the Lord.

What do you see as the greatest wants or needs in your life? How have you tried to fill that void? How do you feel knowing that God wants to have a close and intimate relationship with you?

I. Read John 5:1–6.

How did people at the pool of Bethesda experience healing? How many people were waiting for healing? Why do you think Jesus singled out this particular person to talk to?

What did Jesus already know about his man? How long had the man been ill? Imagine what daily life was like for him. What must his illness have meant for himself and for his family and friends? What was possibly wrong with him? How does his experience mirror what some persons who are disabled go through today?

What question did Jesus ask the man? Why do you think Jesus asked him this? What other times in the Gospels did Jesus ask a perplexing question instead of directly meeting the obvious need?

II. Read John 5:7–10.

How did the ill man answer Jesus' question? What does that tell us about his state of mind and how he saw his situation? What situations have made you feel like a victim? How did you handle being in that position?

What command did Jesus give to the man? How did this command compare to other instructions Jesus gave when healing people? How did the man respond to Jesus' command?

What was the reaction of the religious leaders? Why? Where was their focus? What other passages in the Gospels give evidence of their focus? Describe a situation in the world today in which believers act similarly to the religious leaders. How can legalism impact living in God's grace?

III. Read John 5:11–15.

When questioned by the religious leaders, how did the man respond? What did he know of Jesus right after being healed?

Where did the man go after being healed? Why is this significant? How does this compare to other accounts of Jesus healing people? How do you respond when God provides healing or provision for you?

What instructions did Jesus give to the man? What connection did Jesus seem to make between sinfulness and the man's physical condition? What examples can you think of where someone's sinful choices impacted his or her physical health? While sin is not always the cause of someone's sickness or suffering, how do we tell when it is?

After being challenged by Jesus to consider the state of his heart and to make sure that he did not sin, what did the man do next? Why does this seem like a contrary thing to do? What do you think motivated him to take this action?

Suffering That Teaches

Suffering is unavoidable in this life. Sometimes suffering occurs because of something we did to ourselves or because of a poor decision we made. The consequences of those actions can bring suffering to our physical bodies, our emotional health, and even our relationships with others. There are other times we do not do anything to bring suffering into our lives. Sometimes the journey of suffering we have to deal with is outside of our control (John 9). There is no one to blame for that suffering and we have to press through it, asking for the Lord to strengthen and comfort us. As 1 Peter 4:19 reads, "Those who suffer according to God's will should commit themselves to their faithful Creator and continue to do good." We have to remember that Christ endured great suffering, too; he is our model and example.

How has suffering changed you? What lessons have you learned through suffering? How was God present throughout?

Help Is Available

A victim is someone who has been attacked, robbed, killed, cheated, injured, or fooled by someone else. Even people who have avoided a physical attack have likely been the victim of a joke, a prank, or a harsh comment. Some people develop a "victim mentality." No matter what the situation, they believe they are being attacked. They believe that someone is out to get them, and their constant complaining and blaming ruins potentially good experiences. In order to not "play the victim," we need to choose not to blame others for our problems, take responsibility for our choices, be aware of the root of our feelings, and learn to say "no" when necessary.

The man at the pool of Bethesda most certainly felt sorry for himself. He needed others and was dependent on them. Over thirty-eight years of illness, this perspective had sunk deep into his spirit and made him feel that he was beyond help—a victim of his circumstances.

How did Jesus asking, "Do you want to get well?" address the man's state of being a victim? How do we know when we are failing to take responsibility for our circumstances or when divine help is necessary?

Cheer Up!

The key to looking beyond our circumstances is gratitude. When we remember the many blessings we have and what wonderful things God has done for us, it helps keep us from despair and discouragement. So many challenging situations face us every day, but if we can focus on the good things God has done then we can meet those challenges with courage and even joy.

Although it does not specifically say it in today's text, many commentators agree that the man talked with Jesus again on the same day of his healing. They believe it is possible that the man directly went to offer a sacrifice to the Lord, giving thanks for the miracle he had just experienced. He had been sick for so long, and he was likely experiencing overwhelming emotion at being whole again. Perhaps his encounter with Jesus and the healing miracle that he experienced were an inspiration for living his remaining days to their fullest.

What are you thankful for? Do you live with a spirit of gratitude, with your mind continually focused on what God has done for you? How can you help foster a spirit of gratitude in yourself and in those around you?

Closing Prayer

God, thank you for all you have done for us. You have given us the ability to live victoriously in all circumstances, even the most difficult ones. You have given us your presence, strength, and comfort, and we can find great joy as we think about your many blessings. Help us to be responsible for our own decisions and actions. Help us to choose your way and submit to you. Thank you for the joy that you give us. Amen. ■

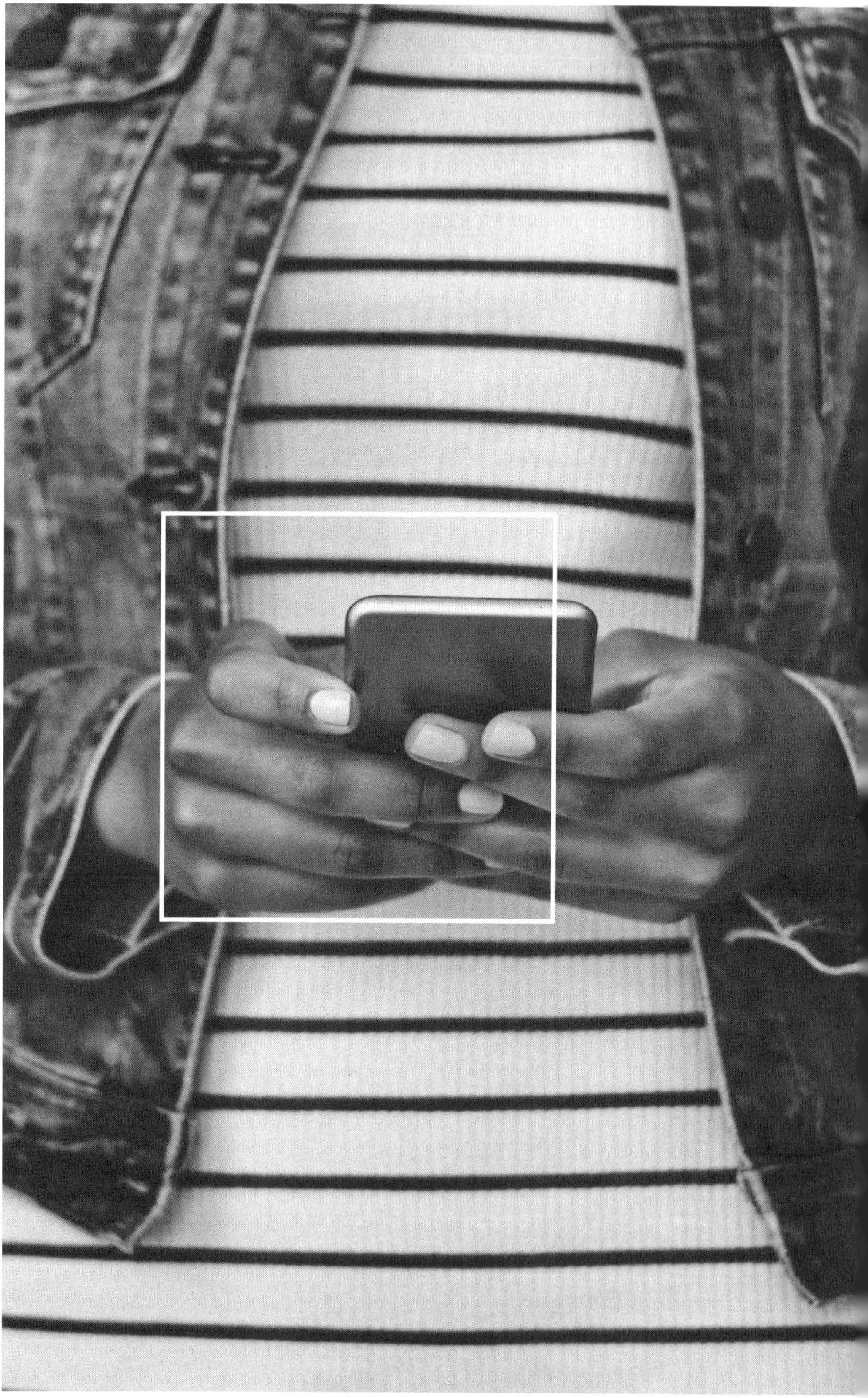

L3

The Danger of Comparison

Genesis 29:16–35; 30:1–24

Main Point

Comparison can lead to discontentment and harmful behaviors.

Background

Jacob was a man of deception. From his youngest years, he tricked others. This was the way he related to people and how he manipulated situations for his own benefit. Eventually deception came back to bite him, as Laban did not honor his agreement with Jacob and pulled a "bait and switch" on Jacob's wedding night. This deception resulted in animosity between sisters Rachel and Leah and dissension between Jacob and Rachel, and it even had long-term consequences in future generations. Rachel and Leah began a journey of comparison, vying for their husband's love and affection, and this impacted the rest of their lives and the lives of their children.

The Comparison Game

It all starts with comparison. *Look at what he has accomplished. Look at what her family does. Look at what they have earned. Look at where they have been.* This comparison leads to covetousness, or the desire to have what someone else has. It leads to dissatisfaction with the gifts and blessings God has given. We develop the feeling that we do not have enough, that something is missing or lacking. Our lives seem incomplete, and if we could just have *that* then surely we would be satisfied! The dissatisfaction that comes from comparison can breed jealousy and will lead us to focus on the wrong things. Instead of feeling gratitude, we are frustrated. Instead of being loving, we are hateful. Instead of being selfless, we are selfish. Instead of focusing on God, we focus on ourselves. Comparison is the place where it all begins.

How often do you compare yourself to others? What has been the result of comparison in your own life? Can it ever be a positive thing? If so, how?

I. Read Genesis 29:16–30.

How does the text describe the physical difference between Rachel and Leah? How did Jacob feel about Rachel? What did Jacob agree to do in order to be married to Rachel?

How did Laban deceive Jacob? How did Jacob feel about it, as evidenced by the passage? How do you think Leah felt about the situation? How do you think Rachel felt?

How did Jacob feel about his wives in comparison to each other? What kind of emotional impact do you think this had on them? How would Jacob's feelings have impacted Rachel and Leah's relationship with each other?

II. Read Genesis 29:31–35.

What did God notice about Leah? What does this tell you about God's character?

What did God do for Leah? Why was this significant?

What do the names Leah chose for her sons indicate? What do they tell us about the state of her heart and her desires?

III. Read Genesis 30:1–24.

Why was Rachel discontent, even though she was loved the most? What did she want? Although God is the giver of good gifts, including children, who did Rachel complain to? Why?

How did Jacob respond to Rachel's plea? Where did he direct her focus?

Compare and contrast the plea of Rachel to have children and Hannah's plea for a son (1 Sam 1). How did they act differently? What was the result of their behavior?

What solution did Rachel come up with when she did not get what she wanted? Who else in the Old Testament took such a step? How did it work out? What happens when we try to solve our own problems instead of taking them to God?

What do the names that Rachel chose for Bilhah's children indicate about her state of mind and her relationship with her sister?

How did the contest between Rachel and Leah continue? What bargains did they strike and why?

Write down below meanings for the names of each of Leah's and Rachel's children (their own and those of their servants). What do you learn about the journey of these sisters, their relationship with each other, their relationship with Jacob, and their relationship with God? What is the significance of these meanings for the future of these children?

Leah	Rachel
Reuben __________	Dan __________
Simeon __________	Naphtali __________
Levi __________	Joseph __________
Judah __________	
Gad __________	
Asher __________	
Issachar __________	
Zebulun __________	

Consider the text of Deuteronomy 21:15–17. What influence could Jacob's situation have had on the development of such a code for the Israelites?

It's Hard to Wait!

Have you ever had a problem that was very challenging, and you asked God to provide a solution but did not hear an answer? What did you do in that moment of uncertainty? Did you continue to wait on the Lord in an attitude of prayer or did you try to find your own solution? It is especially hard to wait on God's answer when we are in turmoil and agony and need help. Rachel felt that she was losing her husband's affection and attention as her sister bore him child after child. Although Jacob loved Rachel most, she was insecure due to having to share her husband with another woman. She expressed her distress to Jacob, but God was silent to her plight and she remained barren. Waiting and seeing her sister's joy was painful and was more than she could bear. Instead of calling out to the One who knew and loved her, she took matters into her own hands, giving her servant to her husband.

Describe a time when you tried to solve a problem on your own instead of waiting on God's timing. How did it work out? What did you learn in the process?

When You're Unloved

Love, affection, and attention are some of the greatest human needs; we crave them with every fiber of our being. But human beings cannot love us completely in the way God does. Human affection and love always fall short and disappoint, but still we seek them. We try to fill the empty spaces in our hearts with love from others, and if people don't love us enough we try to "earn" their affection by giving them what they like, doing favors for them, or being the person they want us to be.

Rachel and Leah were competing for the love of Jacob. Although Jacob was married to Leah first, he loved Rachel. Rachel always had his heart. Leah was unloved and knew she was no match for Rachel. When she was able to get pregnant, she hoped that would earn her husband's love and affection. But no matter how hard she tried to earn Jacob's love, she would never be loved like Rachel.

Describe a time you tried to compete for someone's love and attention or earn someone's affection. How did it work out? What did you learn in the process?

God Knows and Understands

Do you ever feel invisible? Do you ever feel that no one understands what you are thinking and feeling? Do you ever feel overcome by loneliness as you deal with your emotions? Leah was lonely. She was married to Jacob, but just a week after they were married, he married the woman he loved the most. Leah always knew that Rachel was the one Jacob loved. Surely she experienced Jacob's fury at having been deceived. She must have felt his rebuke and reproof as he gave himself completely to the one who had captured his heart. Although Leah was a married woman, she was alone. But God saw her pain. God saw that Leah was unloved, and moved on her behalf. God knew what she felt deep in her heart. Although Leah would never capture the love and attention of her husband, she would be comforted by her many children. God saw her and knew her pain.

How does it encourage you to realize that God knows our feelings and emotions? How does it encourage you to know that God moves on our behalf to bring us comfort? How has God taken care of your heart?

Closing Prayer

Dear God, you are enough for us, but sometimes we do not recognize that. We compare ourselves with others. We struggle with your silence and feel lost and alone. Help us to be aware of you. Help us to realize that your love is enough for us and that you have indeed given us all we need in every situation. Help us to be thankful. Help us not compare ourselves to others but rather give you praise. Amen. ■

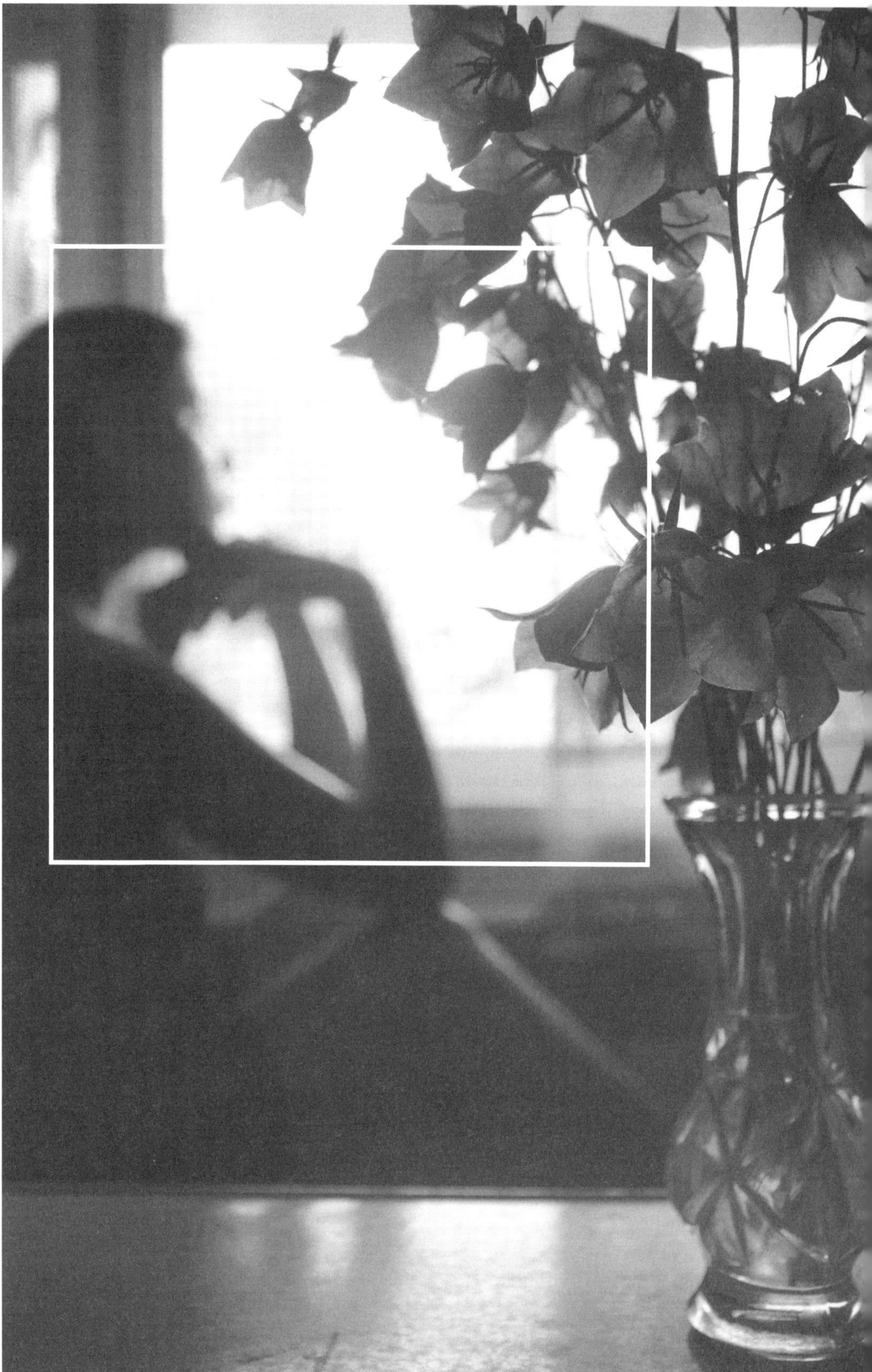

L4

Wrestling with God

Genesis 32

Main Point

We need to wrestle with God to discover who we are.

Background

Years had passed since Jacob and Esau had been in each other's presence. The last time Jacob saw Esau, Esau tricked him out of his birthright and stole his blessing, taking everything he could take from him. Jacob fled to a faraway land where he worked, married, fathered many children, and became successful. His success began to upset others and it was time to return "home." But this meant he would have to face Esau. When Jacob learned that Esau was coming with an army, he was overwhelmed with fear. In preparation for a tumultuous meeting, Jacob ended up in a wrestling match with God.

Taking It to the Mat

Wrestling has a long history. Ancient wall art depicts wrestling moves that are still in use today! The origin of wrestling is most often associated with the Greeks, who made it into an Olympic event. Wrestling adapted further during the time of the Roman Empire. Although there are various types and variations of wrestling today, many of the techniques remain the same. The strongest contender is not always victorious in a wrestling match. To be successful at wrestling requires thought and intention, knowing how to use one's body effectively against an opponent. Some have even compared wrestling to a game of chess. Participants need to anticipate their opponent's next possible move and decisions have to be made accordingly. Wrestling is not just a competition involving brute physical strength; mental strength is important, too.

Describe a time you did something physically challenging that required a great deal of mental strength as well. How did things turn out? What did you learn from the experience?

I. Read Genesis 32:1–2.

Who did Jacob encounter on his journey? How did he respond to this person's presence?

Some scholars suggest that Jacob may have named the area *Mahanaim* ("two camps") because the angels appeared both in front of Jacob and behind him. Look back at Genesis 31. Who was Jacob fleeing from? Who was he preparing to meet? Describe a situation in which you were "surrounded on all sides." How did you manage to make it through? What did you learn from the experience?

In Genesis 31, who told Jacob to take this journey? On the trip, angels were present, surrounding Jacob. How have you been aware of God's presence and protection on your life journey?

II. Read Genesis 32:3–21.

Why do you think Jacob first communicated with Esau via messengers?

What are the details of Jacob's message to his brother? Knowing what you know of Esau's experience with Jacob, how might you feel receiving that message? Describe a time you struggled with forgiving someone who took advantage of you. What helped you with the process of forgiveness?

What information did the messengers bring back? How did Jacob feel when he heard the news? What action did he take first? What was his logic?

What did Jacob ask of God, and why? In the morning, what plan did Jacob implement, and how did he organize it? How many groups did he send on to Esau? Why do you think he did things this way? Describe a time you sought someone's favor or forgiveness with a gift, or received a gift from someone seeking your forgiveness. What was the result?

III. Read Genesis 32:22–32.

What did Jacob do after sending gifts on ahead to Esau? Why do you think Jacob wanted and needed to be alone? Describe a time you sought solitude when facing a difficult situation. What are some benefits and drawbacks of being alone when you are facing tough times, are fearful, or are uncertain how to proceed?

As Jacob was alone, what happened? How long did this continue?

What happened when the next day began to dawn? What did Jacob ask of the man and how did the man reply? Why do you think Jacob asked this?

Through this encounter, what kind of physical change occurred in Jacob? What kind of identity change happened in him? Describe a time you had a "struggle" with God and how the struggle changed you.

The Trouble with Fear

Fear is a mixed bag. Sometimes when we have a bad experience, fear can keep us from repeating a poor choice and hurting ourselves or other people. For example, the fear of harming someone could keep a person from driving while intoxicated. The fear of getting in trouble with the law can help a person follow the rules, or the fear of consequences can help a child learn to make good choices. But for some, fear can be completely paralyzing. The fear of uncertainty can lead people to get stuck and refuse to take any risks in life or in relationships. Fear can keep people from living life to the fullest because they can't move forward in any way. Living in this kind of fear is ignoring the victory that Jesus proclaimed from the cross and the empty grave; it is surrendering to the enemy of our souls; it is ignoring the freedom that we have in our Savior.

What things are you most afraid of? What does fear do to you? How do you work through your fears? How could God help?

Time Alone

Today it is hard to really be alone. The population of the world is increasing and there are few uninhabited places. Population density aside, technology tethers us to constant interaction. With the touch of a button on a smart phone, we can connect to someone via text messaging, voice calling, or even video communication. Most people are highly distracted—in simultaneous conversations with others, reading articles online, and checking out the latest news. It's hard to settle down, to be quiet and spend time with our own thoughts. Something else is always vying for our attention.

Consider trying to "disconnect" for one day. Turn off the cell phone, turn off the radio and television, and don't allow technology to get inside your head. Spend the time communicating with your loved ones, talking to God, and giving your own brain time to think, listen, and create. After this twenty-four-hour exercise, you might write about your experience—what you liked about it, what was challenging, what you learned about yourself.

How often are you alone? What is the benefit of "alone time"? How can we benefit from taking the time to be still in our own minds and still before the Lord?

An Encounter That Changes Us

When we meet God, we are never the same. Jacob was wrestling with God, struggling with God in a moment of doubt and worry. He was very fearful about what was ahead, even though God had given him the instructions to go. He was worried because he knew of the pain and hurt he had caused by deceiving his brother. Jacob had thrived on cheating others—that's who he was. Then, in a pivotal moment, he struggled with God—and it changed his identity. Jacob was transformed from one who clung to deceit into a person who would be the head of the tribes of Israel. The Lord "touched" Jacob's hip to stop the struggle, and this impacted him physically from that point forward. Encounters with God never leave us the same. Jacob left the struggle, ready to face his brother and the challenge that might bring. He left the struggle no longer on a path of deceit, but as a leader.

Describe a time when an encounter with God changed your life. What significant change happened in you?

Closing Prayer

Dear God, thank you for knowing our struggles. Sometimes we need to get alone, face our fears, and wrestle with you to discover who we are and what you desire for our lives. Show us who you are and the plan that you have for us. Help us to put aside our fears. Help us to plan for quiet moments to engage with you, learn from you, and be changed and blessed by you. Amen. ■

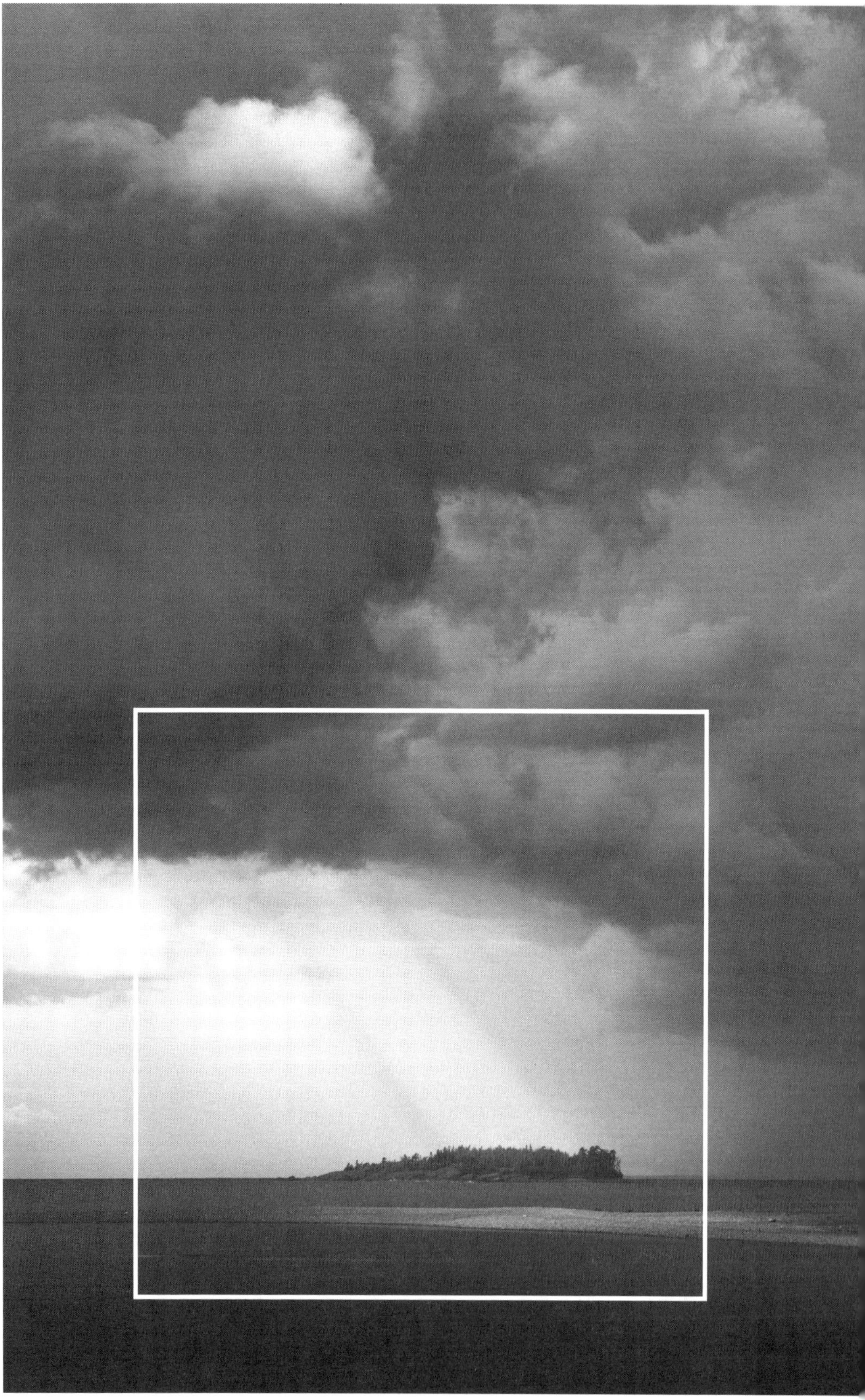

L5

Peace in the Storm

Luke 8:22–25

Main Point

Jesus is the one who can calm any storm in life.

Background

The Sea of Galilee is located in northern Israel. It is about 700 feet below sea level. Historians believe that the point where Jesus and his disciples crossed the Sea of Galilee was about five miles across. Because of the weather and the topography of the surrounding area, this body of water can be subject to surprisingly violent storms. When the wind comes from the east and drops down toward the sea, it meets warm air from the water and can produce fierce weather. Although the disciples were experienced fishermen, even they were challenged by this particular storm. But Jesus was about to do something great.

Stormy Weather

The bigger a boat is and the more passengers and goods it carries, the more secure it tends to be in a storm. Ships today are built to withstand the power of the wind and waves. Technology provides advance warning of potential weather anomalies, and the worst storms have the potential to be avoided altogether. Ships often have wide hulls and may have ballast tanks that provide additional stability. In the time of Jesus, boats were wooden with a mast for sailing, a flat bottom for coming close to shore, and an area for rowing. They were not strong vessels and could easily be capsized by a violent storm. In 1986, archaeologists discovered the remains of a first-century boat that could have been from Jesus' time. This significant find was about twenty-five feet long, seven and a half feet wide, and four feet deep.

If you have you been on a boat in the ocean, describe the experience. If you have ever been in a storm on the sea, what was that experience like? If not, what do you imagine it would be like?

I. Read Luke 8:22–23.

What did Jesus suggest to his disciples? Jesus and the disciples could have gotten to their destination by land; why do you think Jesus opted for a different mode of transportation?

What did Jesus do when they began to sail across the lake? What does this tell us about him?

What happened to the group as they began to sail? What indication do these verses give as to the severity of the storm?

The storm that came was a significant threat to the disciples' safety, but they had an important companion on board. How does it encourage you to know that Jesus is with you on your journey?

Some commentators suggest that this storm was brought about by Satan, to keep Jesus from reaching his destination and accomplishing his purposes. Do you ever feel that you are facing "storms" orchestrated by the Devil himself to bring your downfall and destruction? If so, explain.

How do you think the disciples felt as they tried to keep the boat afloat with their own strength? How do you think they felt about Jesus sleeping through it all?

Jesus did not immediately come to the disciples' aid when the storm started. They were fighting it on their own for a while, but he had not left them. How does that encourage you about going through storms or challenging times?

II. Read Luke 8:24.

What did the disciples end up doing? What about their words indicated that they still did not know Jesus' power?

When Jesus woke, what did he do? What is the difference between "speaking" to the wind and the waves and "rebuking" them? How does this support the idea that Satan orchestrated this storm? What does this tell us about how to respond to Satan's work in our lives?

When Jesus rebuked the storm, what happened? Compare this occurrence with Psalm 107:23–32. What is it like when Jesus calms our storms?

What does this passage teach us about the best way to respond when we are facing storms and troubles?

III. Read Luke 8:25.

What did Jesus ask the disciples after the storm dissipated? Why did he ask this? Although the storm did not bother Jesus at all (it didn't even wake him up), what did bother him? Why should the disciples have had no fear of this storm?

Since we know who Jesus is and the fact that he has overcome the world, how should we face the storms of life?

What response did the disciples have to this miracle? How does this relate to Psalm 107:31? What do you do when God rescues you from the storms that you are facing?

The Power of Storms

Storms can be terrifying. When the Devil is working to challenge you, discourage you, and destroy you, it is hard to hold on to your faith and remember that God already has the victory. Just as the wind in a storm can push a sailor off course, the wind in a storm of life can make us lose our direction and turn our eyes from Jesus. Just as the waves in a storm can engulf a vessel and capsize it with the weight of the water, the waves in a storm of life can crush our spirits and threaten to overwhelm us. Fear can invade because of the storms around us, and we can forget that Jesus is there, walking through each moment with us. We can forget that we have nothing to fear in this life, for he has conquered both death and the grave. Troubles will come, but faith can keep us secure.

What storms have you faced in life? How have you responded to them? How does the story from today's study challenge or encourage you?

Rest and Peace

Jesus was *sleeping* in the boat. He was tired, and this was an opportunity to steal a nap and relax. He needed the rest and rejuvenation before continuing in his ministry. In order for most people to take a nap, they need to have the right conditions. They need to feel sleepy but also have a secure place to sleep—it needs to be quiet and relaxing, and they need to be at ease in order to fall asleep. Jesus fell asleep in the midst of a terrible storm. The pounding waves, the high wind, and the water filling the boat did not disturb him at all. He did not wake up until the disciples shouted and shook him awake. How was he able to be at peace in the midst of the storm? Because of trust. He knew that he was secure against any power of darkness and that he had nothing to fear. We should have that same peace, for Jesus our Savior is victorious.

How have you struggled to find peace? What challenges your peace? What obstacles challenge your trust in God? How can you find rest and peace through Jesus?

Our First Option

What do you do when you face troubles? Do you complain to your family and friends? Do you turn inward and become unsettled, stressed, and depressed? Do you turn to other things to give you solace—drugs, alcohol, sex, or food? Where do you turn when you feel like you have no way out? Where do you head first when the storms of life threaten to overcome you? The disciples did what they could in their own strength, but then they realized that they couldn't handle the situation on their own. We, too, often try to solve things in our own way. We look for human solutions instead of laying it all at the feet of the Savior. Instead of calling on him right away, we struggle—and we often end up hurting ourselves and others in the process. But Jesus will answer us. He will provide a way through, or out. We just need to keep our focus on him.

Have you always gone to the Lord first in times of trouble? Why or why not? What are the greatest challenges to you trusting the Lord? How can you overcome those challenges?

Closing Prayer

God, thank you for demonstrating how to trust and have peace and rest in the midst of the storm. Thank you for always being with us and for responding to our cries for help. When we face overwhelming difficulties, help us turn to you first to find our peace and rest. We give you praise for calming the storms in our lives, and for your loving presence that helps us to face every challenge. Amen. ■

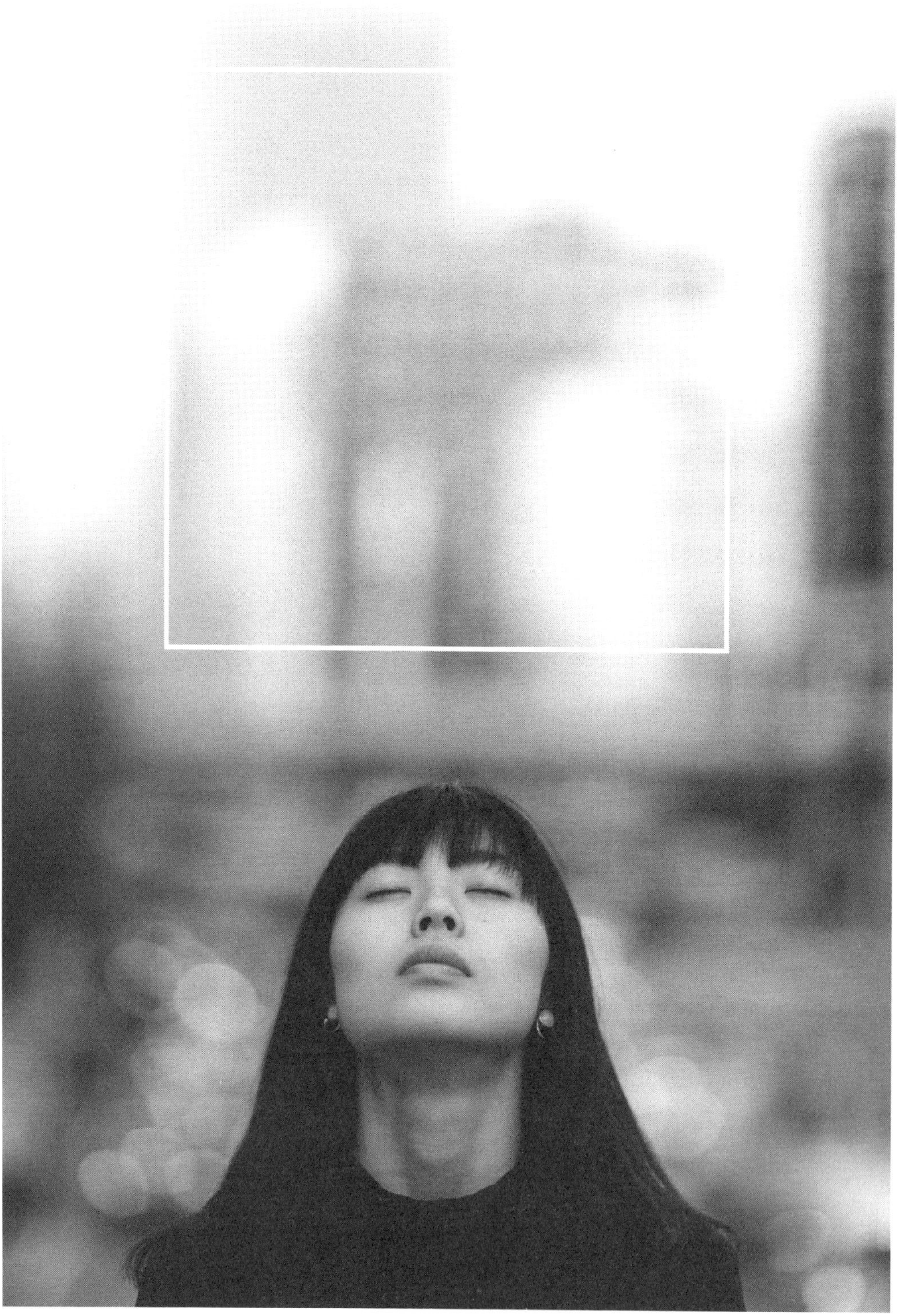

L6

Complete Surrender

Mark 10:17–31

Main Point

Following Jesus requires complete surrender.

Background

Jesus was approached by a man with a great deal of wealth. It seems that this man had more than just wealth, because Luke 18:18 calls him "a certain ruler." In addition to his wealth, the man had power. In the view of society in that day, a person such as this was favored by God. But with Jesus, things are often upside down. Just prior to today's passage, Mark tells us about Jesus blessing children, who had no social status in that culture. While the children were welcomed into the kingdom of God, the rich ruler found the price too high.

How Do I Get In?

Many religions teach that the ability to enter heaven, paradise, or the after life is contingent upon the number of good deeds that you do while you are alive on earth. If your good deeds outweigh your poor choices, you basically earn "points" and are more likely to end up with a positive result when this life is over. Even those who are not particularly religious sometimes describe someone as either a "good" person (follows the rules) or a "bad" person (does morally reprehensible things). But God isn't looking at the number of good choices we make. God isn't interested in how many rules we follow, how many church services we attend, how many dollars we put in the offering plate, or if we go through the right religious steps (Isa 1:11–20). God wants one thing: our completely surrendered and utterly devoted hearts.

What are some things that get in the way of your submission to the Lord? What obstacles keep you from completely giving your heart to God? What do you try to keep control of? Why?

I. Read Mark 10:17–20.

As Jesus journeyed along, who came up to him? How did this person approach Jesus? What does this say about his understanding of who Jesus was?

What did the man ask Jesus? Why do you think he felt the need to ask this?

How did Jesus respond to the man? What was the man's response? What does this tell us about the man?

II. Read Mark 10:21–22.

What does the text tell us about Jesus' feelings for this man? Jesus loves everyone—why would his love be specifically mentioned here?

Jesus did not want to shame the man, embarrass him, or cruelly discipline him. Jesus truly loved him and wanted what was best for him. Describe a time someone asked you to do something that was hard but was for your own good because he or she loved you. How did you respond? Describe a time you asked someone to do something difficult for his or her own good. How did this person react?

When Jesus told the man what he lacked, what was the man's response? What does this tell us about the tension in this man's heart?

Describe a time God asked you to do something that actually grieved you. How did you handle it?

Read what Jesus said in Matthew 6:24. How was this truth proven in the man's life?

III. Read Mark 10:23–27.

How did Jesus address the disciples? Why might he have said this?

What did Jesus say about entering heaven? What analogy did he use?

Some commentators have suggested that Jesus may not have specifically meant a camel but instead was making a play on two similar Greek terms: the word for "camel" and the word for a heavy rope. What was Jesus' point, and how does it remain valid either way?

Who is responsible for who can or cannot enter heaven? Explain.

IV. Read Mark 10:28–31.

What did Peter say to Jesus about what the disciples had done? How did Jesus respond? What did Jesus explain about what it means and looks like to follow him? As Jesus' followers, can we expect good things, bad things, or a mix? Explain. How does this look different from what the world might expect?

If you consider your own heart and life, have you been willing to give up everything to follow Jesus? What have you wanted to hold on to? To what have you given a position greater than Jesus?

Money, Money, Money

Susan's sister-in-law was a yoga instructor overseas and actually instructed some members of the royal family. Since Susan was traveling through, her sister-in-law rescheduled some of her yoga lessons. When the royal family heard that their yoga instructor had family visiting, they graciously invited Susan to the palace. Susan hadn't expected this at all, and it was like nothing she had ever seen! The palace was more beautiful and ornate than words can describe. Three hundred servants waited on the family's every need. The royals she met were warm, kind, and friendly, but she sensed something else as she spent time with them: *They didn't seem happy.* They were some of the richest people on the planet at the moment, but riches cannot truly fufill or satisfy. If someone is missing the source of life, no amount of wealth can buy it.

How have you witnessed wealth, or lack of wealth, impact people? What is the source of greatest fulfillment, and why do so many people miss it?

Giving All

He sat by the offering box, watching. People came flooding in—the rich in their luxuriant robes, those who had less but still enough to live on, and the poor with their wretched clothing. The wealthy put a great deal of money in the box. It was stunning to see how much they gave. These gifts were impressive to most people.

Then she came. She was older, thin and frail, wearing a threadbare wrap. She did not look for attention; in fact, she seemed to be visibly embarrassed. She did not want people to notice her and see how little she was giving. She wanted to be invisible, to disappear. Quietly and without fanfare, she dropped in two coins and drifted away. It was just a couple of coins, but it was all she had.

He saw what she did and it stunned him, because she had given all that she had to live on. Everyone else had given their "extra" as gifts, while she had given everything.

What motivates people to give all they have? What sorts of causes do people support in extravagant fashion? Why can it be difficult for some people to give generously?

Who's In Charge?

When we have everything we think we need, we forget that we are dependent on God for all we have and for who we are. We think that we are in charge, that we are responsible for our success and all we have achieved. However, this is a lie. We are not masters of all we own and do and we are not in control of our own destiny. We are thoroughly and utterly dependent on God. We often learn this when we are at the end of ourselves and have nothing left. Then we see how God is our provider, our source of life, and our sustainer. When our bodies fail, God is our healer. When we don't know where to turn next, God is our guide. It is in those moments when we really recognize our dependency on God that we are living in the truth.

What has helped you realize your dependency on God? How has God provided for you? How has your life been transformed as you have lived in surrender to the Lord?

Closing Prayer

God, everything we have is yours—not only our wealth and possessions but our very lives. When we give ourselves completely to you, we will be changed. Help us to live in total surrender. Help us not to hold on to things that do not fulfill, but to look to you for meaning and purpose. Help us not to chase after wealth, fame, and things that do not last or truly satisfy. You are all we need. Amen.■